THE PURE IN HEART

THE PURE IN HEART

A Study in Christian Sanctity

The Cato Lecture of 1954

by

W. E. SANGSTER
M.A., PH.D. (Lond.)
Minister of The Central Hall, Westminster

ABINGDON PRESS

New York   Nashville

Made and Printed in Great Britain by Butler & Tanner Ltd., Frome and London

TO

PHILIP EDWIN FOUND

IN

AFFECTION AND GRATITUDE

Preface

I WAS MUCH honoured to be invited to deliver the Cato Lecture and can but hope that my volume will not prove altogether unworthy of the series.

The opinions I express are, of course, my own, but I should be an ingrate not to acknowledge the willing help of those with whom I shared my thoughts. I am grateful to the Rev. Eric Kemp, M.A., of Exeter College, Oxford, for conversation and correspondence on canonization in the Anglican Church; for similar help most ungrudgingly given by the Rev. Michael Hollings, M.C., B.A., concerning the Roman Catholic Church; and to my son, Mr Paul Sangster, M.A., who has watched with vigilance both my English and my Greek!

My deeper indebtedness is still harder to express: to my secretary (to whom the book is dedicated) for seeing it through the Press; to Miss Marie Berry, who has been my kind collaborator since I took the work in hand and given most of the leisure of two years to confirming my memory and aiding my research; to my old tutor, the Rev. Dr C. Ryder Smith, who annotated the earlier typescript with scores of useful notes and has always put his wide and exact scholarship at my disposal. Unworthy though the book must be of its high theme, it would have been still more unworthy but for the ready help of these kind friends.

I acknowledge finally the all-pervading aid of my dear wife who makes home a refuge from multitudinous cares and creates that atmosphere in which extra work becomes almost easy and a new call to service just a privilege to grasp.

W. E. SANGSTER

WESTMINSTER

Contents

PART IV
The Path to the Peak
HOW THEY ARRIVED

Introduction

THE PURPOSE of God for man is to make him holy. Not happiness first, and holiness if possible, but holiness first and bliss as a consequence.

But the unreflecting man is not sure that he wants to be holy. He is not certain, to begin with, that he knows what the term means, and he is almost certain that he does not like what he thinks it stands for. To him the word seems musty, and hints at other-worldliness and repression carried to unnatural lengths.

The perplexity of the plain man is not surprising when we remember that the word eludes precise definition even among scholars. Morley remarks, in his essay on Voltaire, that holiness is the 'deepest of all the words that defy definition',[1] but something in the soul of man recognizes and responds to the holy even while he cannot give the concept clear expression. Lacking a neat definition, holiness, none the less, lies at the heart of all devotion. Archbishop Soderblom does not much exaggerate when he says: 'Holiness is the great word of religion; it is even more essential than the notion of God.'[2]

The best way for a man to approach the study of holiness is not first to seek a definition (which is doomed from the start to be inadequate and is almost certain to imprison him), but to gaze steadily and long at those in whom, by general consent, this quality appears, and then to consult his own heart and mind on the reactions which he feels. Let him gaze most of all at Jesus Christ. Let him examine the lives of the saints. Let him think on those obscure disciples he has met on the road of life who seemed always to have the breath of God about them. Let him be unhurried and teachable.

And he will then find that, so far from holiness repelling him, it will fascinate and awe and subdue him. Adoration will stir in his soul. He will wonder at all God can do with human nature and sink to his knees in marvel and surprise. Unutterable longings will awake in him and he will catch himself shaping the question : 'Even me?'

He will realize now that what he had previously supposed to be holiness or saintliness was a caricature of the real thing, and that, in time past, he had grievously misused the word 'saint'. Sometimes he

[1] p. 242 (edn. 1919).　　[2] *Encyclopaedia of Religion and Ethics*, VI.731.

had used the word too *cheaply*, as when he had employed it of anyone who avoided bawdy stories and was of an amiable disposition. Sometimes he had used it too *negatively*, as when he had said, of a puritanical friend: 'He doesn't drink, he doesn't smoke, he doesn't swear, he doesn't joke. He is almost a saint.' Sometimes he had used it *derisively*, as when, in the company of worldlings, to prove that he also was a 'regular fellow', he had announced with gusto that he was 'no saint'.

How cheap and shallow all these uses seem with real holiness in view! The more a man gazes at perfection in Christ, the more he dwells on the approximation to it in the saints; the more he revives the memories of those who, in the circle of his own acquaintances, come nearest to this lovely synthesis of all the virtues, the more it haunts, and holds, and draws him.

Few studies are more rewarding than a study of the saints.

Their experience lies at the heart of all vital religion. Every sincere and thoughtful believer has questioned his own mind at times on what lives at the centre of his faith; what is beyond custom and what is within ceremony; what he would die *for* and what he could die *on*. He would be a poor soul who has not had his moments of revelation; seen, as it were, into the heart of things; touched the Reality which Appearance sometimes reveals and sometimes distorts. Such glimpses are real enough, but, alas, they are fleeting. 'Thoughts, feelings, flashes, glimpses come and go.' The clouds of sense close over and it is gone.

But the believer knows enough to realize, in the company of the saints, that they see steadily what he barely glimpses. Listening to their testimony, he knows that they speak with intimacy of what he understands only in part. He sees them to be masters in a sphere where, though he has hardly served an apprenticeship, he is, at least, in the succession. Like some poor dauber standing before a canvas of Botticelli, he is abased at the poverty of his own work, but boldly claims to be a painter, too! He knows the difficulties the master conquered. He sees with Botticelli's eye. He knows that the vision of beauty which beckons him on is no illusion, but an insight into Reality. Though he is more sure than ever of his own poor workmanship, he picks up his palette and goes on.

All this—and more—the saints do for the simplest servants of Jesus Christ. Though they come (in these centuries of divided Christendom) from different Communions, they speak in essentials with one voice. They both remind us of our lost unity and anticipate its recovery. No man, hard-buffeted in the stress of life, need feel ashamed for leaning, not only on his Lord, but, also, on the example of the saints.

Not only do the saints nourish the faith of simple believers but they speak to the world's need, and they often speak with startling relevance to the times.

Man's chief problem is with himself. Scaling the unscaled mountain, feeding the hungry multitudes of the Far East, finding the cure of cancer, are all small beside the problems which centre in man's chronic selfishness, his erratic will, and his lustful nature.

Can human nature be changed?

Many people outside the Church deny it, and not a few within the Church doubt it. There are theologians who argue that God can do nothing with sin but forgive it, and see the warfare of the Holy Spirit in the human soul as a long-drawn-out guerrilla struggle, never really ended by victory, but only by death.

They do not doubt the *mercy* of God. They exult in His mercy. What they doubt is His ability or willingness to change human nature as we have it here. When the pessimism of the world expresses itself in uncertainty as to whether human nature can be changed, these believers cannot resolve the doubt. They doubt themselves.

The saints can resolve the doubt. They do it less by argument than by example. Can human nature be changed? It has been done! Again and again. The worst made the best; the lowest lifted to the highest. Lust conquered; self dethroned; all life, a life of love.

The question whether human nature can be changed will never be settled by argument. It demands another kind of proof.

The saints provide the proof.

Worldlings know little of the lives of the saints and laugh at the little that they know, but the saints are speaking to the world's need. Every other problem is minor beside this—Can man be changed? If men cannot be changed they will destroy themselves.

Surprising as many people would find the statement, a study of the saints is not a byway of scholarship, or the hobby of hagiographers, but the nourishment of hope in a dark world. The saints are answering the question the world most wants to know. Man can be changed.

Nor does the service of the saints end even here. They often speak, we have said, with startling relevance to the times.

One day, in the Grand Jury Room of the Southern District of

New York, Whittaker Chambers was giving evidence in the case of Alger Hiss. A juror leaned forward and asked him: 'Mr Chambers, what does it mean to be a Communist?' Chambers thought a moment and then exposed the spring of his forsaken loyalty. He explained that when he was a Communist, he had three heroes: a Russian, a Pole, and a German Jew.

The Pole was Felix Djerjinsky, later to be head of the Tcheka and organizer of the Red Terror. As a young man, he had been a political prisoner in the Paviak Prison in Warsaw. In the Paviak Prison in Warsaw, Djerjinsky *insisted* on cleaning the latrines of the other prisoners. The most developed member of any community, he held, must take upon himself the lowliest task.

That was one thing, Whittaker Chambers explained, that it meant to be a Communist.

The German Jew was Eugen Leviné. He organized the Workers' and Soldiers' Soviets in the Bavarian Soviet Republic of 1919. When the Republic was suppressed, Leviné was captured and court-martialled. The court came to its inevitable conclusion. 'You are under sentence of death,' they told him. Leviné answered: 'We Communists are always under sentence of death.'

That was another thing, Whittaker Chambers explained, that it meant to be a Communist.

The Russian was a pre-Communist named Sazonov. Arrested for a part in the plot to assassinate the Csarist Prime Minister, von Plehve, he was sent to one of the worst prison camps in Siberia, where the political prisoners were flogged unmercifully. Sazonov wondered how he could bring this wickedness to the notice of the world. At last he found a way. Choosing his time, he drenched himself in kerosene, set himself alight, and burned himself to death.

And that also, Whittaker Chambers explained, is what is meant to be a Communist.[3]

No one can answer this kind of challenge but the saints. Conventional religion is powerless. It cannot do it. It does not deserve to do it. Such passion and self-sacrifice cannot be outmatched in a moral world by religion which has made terms with Mammon. Who can doubt that one reason why the Christian religion has not been more influential in the world is because the spirit of the world has invaded the Church? We have professed the faith and not lived it. We have talked of humility and sacrifice, but in our hearts we

[3] *Witness*, pp. 5 f.

have shrunk from them. We have lived to see militant atheists stagger us with the utterness of their self-giving.

Only the saints can answer this heroic unbelief.

Each of these deeds of splendid abasement and sacrifice is paralleled and surpassed by the servants of God. They will do as much as Djerjinsky, Leviné, and Sazonov did—and *do it for their enemies.* They will sacrifice all that they have (their life included) *and do it with only love in their hearts.* The revolution they would work in the world would leave no legacy of hate and create no counter-revolution. Their way—because it is the way of God—would bring heaven to earth, and it can come no other way.

The saints speak to the problems of the Church as well as to the problems of the world. The more the saints *of* all Communions are known *in* all Communions, the sooner will the dismembered body of God be made whole again. They would lift the standard of common life among all Christians. God would use them to bring revival. They, more than anybody else, would make the Church challenging to the world.

So we set out on our study of sanctity with these hopes in our heart.

We must inquire first how man became aware of the holy: what was *different* in it, and what was fascinating about it; whether it is for all.

We must trace the growth of this apprehension of the holy through the Scriptures and into the history of the Church, observing how the term 'saint' narrowed from its wide New Testament use to describe only those whose virtue was of heroic proportions. The tests of sanctity in the various branches of Christendom must come under our review, and we must notice why, in one section of the Universal Church, there are no tests of sanctity at all.

What the saints are really like, and how they came to such sublime stature, will conclude our task.

Some readers of the book, especially those (if I have them) of the non-Protestant world, will think that the term 'saint' as applied to Protestants is too vague to be of use. Some vagueness, I admit, attaches to it. Where there are no clear rules of canonization, inevitably the term 'saint' ceases to have sharp edges. But, then, something of imprecision attaches to the term wherever it is used, even in the Roman Church. Through much more than half of Christian history, there were no central and clear-cut tests. Of many, many

early saints we know nothing but the name. Others—like the ill-
tempered St Jerome—were canonized more for their service than
for their sanctity.[4] Needle-sharpness is not possible in the use of
this term.

Our study will not involve us in a discussion of the invocation of
the saints, or require the expression of any opinion on levitations,
transports, and trances. It is conceded today that these latter
phenomena sometimes have a non-Christian origin.[5]

Little will be said about miracles, or the use of relics, not because
I do not believe that elements of the miraculous are associated with
the saints, but because all hagiographers agree that many old
chroniclers exaggerated to the glory of God (!) and it is difficult now
to distinguish the truth in the wonder-tales. Perhaps nothing is more
miraculous in this evil world than a holy life itself. It cannot be
reduced to 'mere ethics'. It flames with the supernatural.

People who can find God only in their own segment of Christendom will find little to delight them here. I have learned to love
sanctity wherever it can be found. I regard it as a major misfortune
that the different branches of the Universal Church know so little
of each other's saints. One of the happy, easy tasks for anyone who
has the willingness and capacity for it, is to open the treasures of
spirituality in one Communion to those who worship in another.
Not soon will I forget the almost tearful gratitude of a man, thirty-
four years a member of the closed section of the Plymouth Brethren,
when I guided his reading in the saints of the Middle Ages. 'I had
never so much as heard of St Francis of Assisi,' he said. Nor can I
forget, either, the almost dumb wonder and thankfulness of a devout
Roman Catholic in being made free of Charles Wesley's hymns.

Those who are intimate with God have a way of conquering us,
almost against ourselves. More than thirty years ago, Monsignor
R. A. Knox began to write a book on ultrasupernaturalism which
was to include 'a kind of rogues' gallery', and prominent in the
rogues' gallery he had a place for John Wesley.[6] But the years went
by and the more he got to know his 'rogues' the less rogue-like they
became. In the end, he concluded that his difference with them was
in the placing of an emphasis.[7] He had become eager only to understand them and not to prove them wrong.[8]

[4] *Encyclopaedia Britannica* (14th Edn.), XIII.3.
[5] cf. Thurston, *The Physical Phenomena of Mysticism.*
[6] *Enthusiasm*, pp. v f.　　　[7] ibid., p. 590.　　　[8] ibid., p. vi.

Much in this study should be searching and humiliating. Though hagiographers approach their work in different ways, one writing only panegyric and another questioning all things, they have this quality in common—they never imagine that they are saints themselves. They live too much with the truly advanced to cherish illusions of their own holiness.

But they follow after!

This book aims to help others who would follow after.

First, then, how did man become aware of the holy and how did his longing for holiness grow?

What tests have been shaped through the centuries to decide who were heroic in virtue?

What is a saint really like?

How did he become such?

Those are the questions which must engage us now.

PART I

The Development of the Idea of the Holy

IS SANCTITY ONLY FOR THE FEW?

CHAPTER I

Before the Testaments

A SENSE of the holy is far older than all the great religions. By the time the great religions took shape man was using clear concepts. The Deity was thought of as being Spirit possessing Power, Reason and Will. The greater the religion, the richer its clear ideas. The development of religion is largely a development of its *thought*. It has grown in rationality. Dogmas have been rough-hewn, then shaped and, at the last, finely chiselled. Theology has become a science. Some of the debates that went to the shaping of the creeds can be followed only by philosophers.

Nor would the student of religion regret this if religion in some eras had not become intellectually lopsided. There is more in the religious consciousness than can ever go into concepts. It is generally conceded now that the non-rational has a contribution to make as well as the rational. The arrogance of supposing that, what could not be clearly expressed could be cheerfully discarded, has impoverished religion and made lonely men of its mystics and seers. So far from it being a mark of greater intellectual grasp to press only along the rational path, it was, in some ways, the path of least resistance. One had at least the help of language. The things discarded would not go into words and how can one discuss what will not go into words?

But perhaps it is only *precise* words into which they will not go. Mystics and seers are not normally dumb. If they preach the virtues of silence, they do so like Carlyle—'in thirty volumes'. Primitive man was aware of more things than he could put into clear concepts and the devout soul has been in that situation ever since. Religion has many inexpressible experiences. Indeed, those experiences may prove the unique contribution of the religious consciousness to man's understanding of himself and his world. To deny the contribution to religion of all which will not go into precise terms, is to equate the Deity with human ideas of His attributes, whereas those attributes are but predicates of the Sublime, Who is infinitely beyond their power fully to express, much less to encompass, and never to exhaust.

Throughout the whole of our inquiry this contribution of the non-

rational must be borne in mind. Clearly, we do not mean the irra-
tional. But, just as man knows only the skin of the sea and a few
hundred feet beneath it, but is aware that the ocean is over six miles
deep in places, and that the vast unexplored depths constantly affect
the shallow area of his knowledge, so the religious thinker knows that
beneath the area of ordered thought there is a vast ocean of which
he cannot speak in clear terms and with detailed understanding but
of which he feels the pull, and knows the effect, and from which he
enjoys experiences he cannot put into plain words.

And this may help us towards the end of our road when we face
the fact that saints even *think* in a different way from philosophers:
that meditation and not logical reasoning is their approach to truth
and that adoration lends them power to dive where logic cannot go.
Scientific men used to smile at Pascal's assertion that 'the heart has
reasons of which the head has no knowledge' and decline to admit
that thought can proceed on images as well as on ideas.

Yet it can. One can go by plane as well as by car. If, at the last,
we conclude that there *is* something unusual in the way saints appre-
hend, we shall remember that we met at the outset of our study this
contribution of the non-rational to the idea of the holy, and must
keep in mind that there are other paths to knowledge than the path
of logical thought.

Certainly, our study begins before the emergence of clear ideas.
Primitive man felt himself to be in a world in which he stood over
against a threefold 'otherness': (i) things, (ii) other men, (iii) Something or Someone high and eerie.[1] It is with his awareness of this
Something or Someone that we have to do, and our aim is to isolate,
in particular, one element that we shall find there—the 'germ' of
the holy.

The most illuminating study of this question in our time is the
work of Dr Rudolf Otto. He asserted that 'Holiness is a category of
interpretation and valuation peculiar to the sphere of religion'.[2] In
the development of man's thought it gets transferred to ethics but
it is not derived from ethics. It includes 'a quite specific element or
"moment" which sets it apart from the rational'—i.e. makes it impossible for the mind to grasp in terms of clear ideas. An analogy
may be found in a quite different sphere—the category of the beautiful. A sunset cannot go into a syllogism.

[1] cf. Ryder Smith, *The Bible Doctrine of Man*, p. 39.
[2] *The Idea of the Holy* (E.T.), p. 5.

In common use today Holiness means 'absolutely good', but that use is derived. If the word originally included the seed idea of moral perfection (and that would be debated) it was not the only element and it was not the chief. Another was present, more primitive and more prominent. For this other element, Otto felt the need of a new name and adopted a word coined from the Latin *numen*. *Omen* had given us *ominous*: *numen* could give us *numinous*. He holds that 'this mental state is perfectly *sui generis* and irreducible to any others; and, therefore, like every absolutely primary and elementary datum, while it admits of being discussed, it cannot strictly be defined'.[3]

This element lives in all real religion. It is in the Hebrew *qadosh*, in the Greek ἅγιος, and in the Latin *sacer*. All these terms have come to connote ethical excellence, but they were not ethically excellent in origin and, even today, could they be robbed of the numinous element, something precious in them would perish. They would pass from the realm of the spiritual to become terms of interest only to moralists.

If a man has no sense of the numinous there is not much one can do about it. Only God can open the eyes of the blind. Preachers in all ages, seeking to express the inexpressible and consciously failing, have said with Myers's *St Paul*:

> *Oh could I tell ye surely would believe it!*
> *Oh could I only say what I have seen!*
> *How should I tell or how can ye receive it,*
> *How, till He bringeth you where I have been?*

Yet one can do a little. One can *try* to say it. One can draw analogies from other realms of thought. One can put a man in the place where others have seen it. One can encourage oneself with the knowledge that 'the Father seeketh such'[4] and that it is highly doubtful if any man ever went through life without a gleam.

But more than this one cannot do. It is not taught, or explained, or expressed in a formula. Those who 'attend' to the Spirit are 'quickened'.

When Otto came to analyse the numinous, he paid tribute to Schleiermacher for isolating the 'feeling of dependence' in this experience, but criticizes him under two heads.

First, because Schleiermacher made his 'feeling of dependence'

---

[3] *The Idea of the Holy* (E.T.), p. 7.   [4] Jn 4$_{23}$.

differ from the feeling of dependence we have in other realms of life only in degree, whereas it is a difference of intrinsic quality. The two states of mind are clearly distinguished introspectively. This abasement before the Great Other is 'only definable through itself' just because it is 'so primary and elementary a datum of our physical life'. Otto names it 'creature-consciousness'. It is 'abasement into nothingness before an overpowering absolute might.'[5]

Secondly, he criticizes Schleiermacher because Schleiermacher argued that we only come to the fact of God as the result of an inference. Having a 'feeling of dependence', man posits a cause for it.

The psychological data do not bear this out. Indeed, they testify to the contrary. Creature-consciousness is a concomitant and, at the same time, a consequence of another feeling-element 'which casts it like a shadow' and which is begotten by the numinous felt as objective and outside of the self.

We have spoken of 'analysing' the numinous, but the word 'analyse' is too concrete. The nature of the holy can best be hinted at by looking at the feelings it begets in the mind. Let anyone who knows in experience what it is to have commerce with heaven think his way to the heart of his awareness and he will find what Otto calls *mysterium tremendum*: a feeling sometimes serene and sometimes volcanic; sometimes ecstatic and sometimes adoring. Charles Wesley tried to say it in a hundred ways and this among them:

> *The speechless awe that dares not move*
> *And all the silent heaven of love.*

It is in this dim awareness in the primitive mind of man that we who understand the origins of the holy must work. Even for the Christian, to begin with the Bible is to begin too late.

Passing *tremendum* first, through his prism, Otto distinguished three elements in it. The elements of Awe-fulness, of Overpowering-ness, and of Energy.

There is common agreement that primitive man knew an unearthly dread. It was no ordinary dread. It was not fear of other men; not even of *hosts* of other men: nor of wild beasts who disputed a cave with him. It was different in kind. It was shuddering and eerie and awe-ful. It was the realm of *mana* and *tabu*.

But notice—'the awe-ful' is still present in those lines of Charles

[5] op. cit., p. 10.

Wesley just quoted: sublimated, adoring, and mute. We see in the unearthly dread of primitive man the seed and the soil from which that noble abasement sprang. The sublimest adoration of the saint is but the long refinement of that early awe.

To the element of the Awe-ful is added 'Overpoweringness' ('*majestas*').

A gleam of the numinous still lies upon the word 'majesty'. Who cannot feel the unutterable majesty and overpoweringness of the King of Kings, the Lord of Lords, and only Ruler of Princes? 'The Lord', says the Psalmist, 'sitteth as King for ever.'[6]

Charles Wesley says it for us again:

> *The o'erwhelming power of saving grace,*
> *The sight that veils the seraph's face; . . .*

O'erwhelming . . . and the veiled seraphs! The seed and the soil of this holy adoration are both in the awareness of the numinous in early man.

To the Awe-ful and the Overpowering is added Energy.

At the heart of the sense of the holy, early man discerned a pulsating *activity*. Even before the era of the great religions begins, our primitive forebears knew that the Great Other *did things*. Power resided at the heart of the Mysterious. It was with a *living* God that early man felt himself in contact.[7]

Those who would replace the God of religion with the Absolute of philosophy know that the battleground is here. Those who still believe in a Living God, and seek to read in the events of their own time the righteous sentence of the Almighty on the conduct of men, will feel their kinship with primitive man who sensed also, in his dim way, the urgent Energy at the centre of that Something or Someone with whom 'he had to do'.

Otto slips into an examination of *mysterium* quoting Tersteegen: 'A God comprehended is no God.'

And God is not comprehended. He is the 'Great Other'. Mysteriousness and awe-fulness are not to be equated. A piece of machinery I do not understand is not strictly 'mysterious' to me. It is, at present, beyond me. I cannot grasp it now. It is a problem in that sense but not (with an exact use of words) *mysterious*—for some understand it.

[6] Ps 29_{10}. [7] cf. Snaith, *The Distinctive Ideas of the Old Testament*, p. 48.

But the numinous is *mysterium*—absolutely and for ever beyond my comprehension. Not beyond my approaching—but beyond my comprehension. 'A God comprehended is no God.' Nothing can give adequate expression to this remoteness in accessibility. 'Transcendent' is the word theologians use, and 'supernatural' perhaps, the plain man. Both will serve though neither is adequate. As so often in these dim borderlands, we deeply feel and cannot clearly say.

Fascination is another element in the holy. In the combination of daunting and fascination Otto finds 'the strangest and most noteworthy phenomenon in the whole history of religion'.[8] For primitive man the daemonic-divine object allured and repelled: charmed and terrified: held and yet utterly abashed. The daunting probably preceded the fascination.

To master the mysterious, primitive man employed magic. He wanted to use the power of God *for his own ends*. But not—in the history of the race—for long. To have God and 'to be had' by Him, became an end in itself. Remote ages dimly anticipated the cry of the saint: 'It is not Thy gifts that I desire: it is Thyself.'

In this soil grew the seed of some of the strangest and some of the most beautiful plants in the garden of humanity. To what amazing lengths have men and women gone to prepare their hearts as a dwelling place of the divine! To have *God*: to be possessed by the Spirit: to be indwelt . . . ages and ages before THE LORD GAVE THE WORD in Christ men aspired. All the rigours of asceticism, the fastings and floggings and macerations and brandings, all for this.

And the possibility of response to this fascination is in *all* men. 'Thou hast formed us for Thyself, and our hearts are restless till they find rest in Thee.' There is the ground of our hope: that, when we weary of the things of earth, we shall turn to Him in Whom alone we can find rest for our souls.

In its climacteric moments the response to fascination brims over. This is the 'overaboundingness' of which the mystics speak and which we shall meet again and again in our study. Teresa of Avila knew it and, having known it, longed to die: did, indeed, die of it at the last. She succumbed to no normal illness; it was 'the inextinguishable flame of Divine Love which caused her death'.

In seeking to isolate the non-rational element in the idea of the holy we had need to set aside the strictly ethical, and suggested that ethics belonged to later stages of thought: or was present in the

[8] op. cit., p. 31.

primitive mind (if at all) in 'germ'; and, in any case, was not our chief concern here.

But we are moving on to examine the idea of the holy in the Old Testament and, therefore, to a maturer stage of development, and the question of how the ethical appeared in the numinous may be anticipated.

In this connexion Otto dislikes the phrase 'gradually evolved'— and not merely the phrase: he contests the idea. The appearance of the moral 'ought' in man is said by many to have its origins in the constraint of the herd: that the custom of the clan 'gradually evolved' into the moral imperative. How it so evolved is not explained.

Can it be explained on these lines? If the content of conscience is what society approves, did conscience itself arise in the same way? Otto does not think so. He holds that ' "ought" has a primary and unique meaning, as little derivable from another as blue from bitter. . . .'[9] 'The idea "ought" is only "evolvable" out of the spirit of men itself, and then in the sense of being "arousable" because it is already potentially implanted in him. Were it not so, no "evolution" could effect an introduction for it.'[10]

He holds rather that feelings like ideas are associated and can excite each other but that, so far from the custom of the clan 'evolving' (or being transmuted) into a personal and commanding and deeply-felt 'ought', the connexion is to be sought rather in the association of feelings. It may be, seeing that both the custom of the clan and the moral imperative are constraints upon conduct, that the former aroused the latter in the mind but, if that were so, it aroused what was already potentially planted there and man effected a transition from one to the other. But it was a *replacement* of one by the other, not a *transmutation*. Moral obligation is not derived from any other feeling: it is *sui generis* and unevolvable.

The relation of the rational and the non-rational in the idea of the holy becomes clear at this point. The association of feelings sets up lasting connexions between one emotion and another. The religious and ethical are conjoined in this way and not by mere conjunction but by inward cohesion and affinity. The numinous and the ethical combine like oxygen and hydrogen in water and become indistinguishable in experience. So there emerges the unitary but 'complex category of "holy" itself, richly charged and complete, and in its fullest meaning'.[11] Reason may strain dregs out of the water. This is its great but only office.

[9] op. cit., p. 44.   [10] ibid., p. 45.   [11] ibid., p. 46.

We may go further. We observed that the reaction of the mortal to the numinous was 'creature-consciousness' with its attendant feelings of human littleness and abasement. Another sort of self-disvaluation awakes with this: uncleanness, pollution, profanity. It is marked, when it comes, by an immediate spontaneity. It is not a fruit of deliberation but breaks 'palpitant from the soul'.

To those who know nothing of it, nothing much again can be said. A man must '*see*' the numinous to feel profane. Yet, if we were right in doubting whether any man passes through life without catching a gleam of the numinous, we may doubt also if any man is quite unaware of a sense of uncleanness within.

Men are often unschooled in their own nature, inattentive to what stirs only vaguely within them, and either neglectful or false in their interpretation of experience.

The religious consciousness of men developing through all ages, and awake among all peoples, bears immense testimony to this double apprehension of mortal mind: a judgement of unspeakable *appreciation* on the *numen*, and, in its presence, a judgement of unspeakable *depreciation* on the self. Only the *numen* is truly holy. If the numinous belongs to a few mortals, (and community at its earliest stage included its spiritual leaders), this is merely by reflection. Only God is of transcendent worth and, therefore, *worshipful*: perfect, beautiful, sublime. From the far future we hear the crashing paean of praise: 'Blessing and Honour, Glory and Power be unto Him that sitteth upon the throne.'

But man is dyed in sin, loathsome and polluted. The awe of *tremendum*, when united with the ethical, has unfolded into this. Man needs cleansing, atonement and sanctification.

To the threshold of the great religions—and a little beyond—have we now come.

CHAPTER II

The Old Testament

THERE ARE no sharp divisions in the history of ideas. The development of a concept may cover many centuries and its growth is often neither steady nor constant. At one level of community life, thought may enlarge and soar: at another, in the same generation, it is narrow and primitive. In one era a man of piercing insight will indicate the road his successors may take centuries to lumber along, and, even then, not without some counter-marching. Dating ideas, and their enlargement, must, of necessity, be rough.

The growth of the idea of the holy in the Old Testament illustrates this roughness. The sublimest moments do not appear at the end. A strict application of chronology would only provide 'anachronisms'. The history of events must be used on occasion to explain what appears to be the queer regressions in the history of ideas: how, for instance, a people which had seen holiness in all its ethical grandeur could be deeply concerned again about the 'holiness' of a cultus and the ceremonial purity of *things*. Yet from first to last, the unfolding never fails of interest. Herein, surely, lies the central significance of the Hebrew people: not in their wars and conquests, nor in their pomp and state, nor in all the king's horses nor all the king's men . . . but in their growing understanding of holiness and in their succession of patriarchs, seers and prophets to whom the Holy God chose to reveal Himself.

For therein, as Dr Ryder Smith pertinently remarks, lies the differentia of the Hebrew *qadosh*.[1] This term for holy (and its cognates) appears no less than 605 times in the Old Testament.[2] The long history of the idea in earlier thought we have already traced, and it still has both the daunting and the fascination we should expect but it has this also in Hebrew religion: not only that men are impelled, despite their dread, towards the Holy God, but that the Holy God Himself comes to favoured and selected men.

Genesis 15 sets the scene. The Lord comes. Abram fears. The eyes of the mortal are directed towards the sweeping heavens and all the innumerable stars. The promise is given and the offering

[1] *Bible Doctrine of Man*, p. 40.   [2] ibid., p. 39.

prepared. The pieces of the sundered sacrifice are laid over against each other and Abram steps, we may assume, between them, in token that he is willing himself to be hacked in halves if he breaks the solemn vow.[3]

As the sun sinks to rest, Abram sinks to rest also. And his sleep is very deep.

Indeed, it is more than sleep. 'Lo, an horror of great darkness fell upon him.'

And God spoke the promises again. In the darkness 'behold a smoking furnace, and a flaming torch that passed between the pieces' and God sealed the covenant. He, too, would be held by it. Heaven and earth had entered into contract.

The Old Testament record may begin there. It contains all the elements we should expect from the previous chapter and infinitely more. God is known—at least to one man. He can communicate His meaning to mortal mind. With a selected man He will enter into covenant. He is in awe-ful separation from the human and yet in compact as well. In that horror of great darkness and by that flaming torch our journey can begin.

It will be clearly borne in mind that, in the Old Testament, the Lord *only* is holy. Holy *per se*.

Yet there is a derivable holiness which attaches, (by contact with Him), to things and persons and places and seasons, growing less numinous and less potent as they get further away.

To begin with *things*.

The holy *place* is common in almost all early religions and is common in Israel too.[4] But beneath Sinai, under Divine instruction, Moses erected a Tent of Meeting. It may be that the simple Tent of Meeting which Moses pitched well outside the camp and which had its single non-Levitical servitor in Joshua[5] has been idealized in the description of a later historian into the elaborate Tabernacle set down in the centre of the camp with its host of attendant priests and Levites.[6]

But God chose to dwell there. It was the place of meeting. It contained the ark. It blazed with the true Shekinah. From that burning centre, the numinous streamed out on things and persons. When the Tabernacle turned into the solid stone of the Temple, and the ark found its last resting place there,[7] this became *the* holy place

---

[3] Driver, *The Book of Genesis*, p. 176.   [4] Ex 3₅, 20₂₄. Jos 5₁₅.
[5] Ex 33₇₋₁₁.   [6] Ex 25–7, 30, 31.   [7] 1 K 8₁ff.

of all holy places.[8] Unique! In its innermost shrine—its Holy of Holies—without image and, ultimately, without ark, God dwelt.

> *Who can behold the blazing light?*
> *Who can approach consuming flame?*

From that glowing centre, into which only the high priest entered, a nimbus spread (in theory) over all Israel.[9]

The derivable holiness which attached to things because of their contact with God impregnated the vessels of the cultus,[10] the oil,[11] the incense,[12] the shewbread[13] and the priest's clothing.[14] Dr Ryder Smith[15] takes the view that the offerings of the people (i.e. the sacrifices) were not called 'holy' because they were given *by* man *to* God. But even these did not miss the hallowing of divine contact. At least in one place the very gifts are called 'holy', even though there is an 'iniquity on the holy things'.[16]

From *things* we may turn to *seasons*.

Certain portions of time were set aside as sacred because they belonged in a special way to God. Their sanctity was marked by a limitation of action on the part of His devotees—and some of them by feasting, and some by fasting.

The different phases of the moon usually marked these solemn seasons: the *new* moon especially.[17]

But of all dedicated portions of time none exceeded in frequency or firmness in Israel the observance of the Sabbath.[18] The day was, indeed, a *holy* day, rigidly secured from all secular toil and hedged about with a hundred regulations to preserve its sanctity. God had 'blessed the seventh day and hallowed it'.

From seasons we may turn to *persons*.

Normally priests came highest in the scale of holiness because, by the nature of their office, they came closest in their contact with God. Their sanctity derived less from their quality of life (though they were warned against heavy drinking before they performed their holy offices[19] and against adultery[20]) than from their service of the cultus. It was a ceremonial holiness which was most in mind. They were nearest the Holy of Holies, they handled the hallowed vessels and they wore the sacred robes.

---

[8] Dt 12$_5$.   [9] Is 48$_2$. Zech 2$_{12}$.   [10] Nu 3$_{31}$.   [11] Ex 30$_{25, 33}$.
[12] Ex 30$_{35-7}$.   [13] 1 Sam 21$_5$.   [14] Ex 28$_{2, 4}$. Ez 42$_{14}$.
[15] *Bible Doctrine of Man*, p. 42.   [16] Ex 28$_{38}$.
[17] Amos 8$_5$. Hos 2$_{11}$. Is 1$_{14}$.   [18] Gn 2$_{2f}$. Ex 20$_{8-11}$.
[19] Lev 10$_9$.   [20] Lev 21$_7$.

Nothing more stresses the non-ethical character of holiness among other early peoples nor yet its derivative nature from association with the deity, than the use of this term for the sodomite servants of the holy place and the priestess-prostitutes.[21] Whenever this practice is named in the Old Testament it is denounced. This probably means that it did occur at some Hebrew shrines. Only as the prophets discerned the burning ethical heart of holiness was the practice finally exterminated, only to be remembered with horror.

The Nazarites[22] and the prophets[23] shared with the priests the holiness which belonged to those who served God in special ways.

Yet this holiness did not attach only to those whose service was obviously religious—and religious in a modern use of the word. Kings were holy and warriors going on service were hallowed, as the phrase 'sanctify war' shows.[24] The king was anointed with oil like the priest. He also was a servant of God and separated to service. His office in Israel, like the office of the priest, became hereditary. Yet in neither case was birth alone enough. The one so born must be ceremonially hallowed too.[25] Nor is it surprising, when one remembers the preoccupation of the prophets with national affairs, that those who responded to the call of Israel's God to defend Israel by battle 'in all assaults of her enemies' should share His holiness also. If the word is not used of warriors the implication is there and, for that matter, the *word* is seldom used of priests or prophets. It is so obvious it can be assumed.[26] To say 'Holy priest' and 'holy prophet' would border on the pedantic. Of course they were holy. The office implied it. And when a warrior went forth from Israel as a soldier of the Lord, the implication of holiness attached to him also.[27]

So much, then, for the derivative holiness which attached by contact with God to things and places and seasons and persons. The big question now faces us. What of the growth of the ethical within the ceremonial? How did the moral awake in the ritual, and did it awake to subordinate and then destroy the ritual, or did the ritual rise with it to conserve and express the ethical? Is the numinous element still present, or is there 'awe-ful loss' in the moral victory?

[21] Gn 38$_{21f}$. cf. 1 K 14$_{24}$; 15$_{12}$. Amos 2$_7$. Hos 4$_{11}$.
[22] Nu 6$_{5-8}$.   [23] 2 K 4$_9$. Jer 1$_5$.
[24] Jer 6$_4$ (R.V. margin).
[25] Lev 8.   [26] Ryder Smith, *Bible Doctrine of Man*, p. 48.
[27] Joel 3$_9$. Jer 6$_4$.

Was it a 'rise downwards', with goodness stripped of *mysterium tremendum* and the moral 'ought' rationalized into social obligation? Or do the numinous and ethical elements in the idea of the holy, when blended in the Old Testament, mount to a higher concept which has yet to be revealed?

In the growth of the ethical in the idea of the holy in the Old Testament, the word 'righteousness' plays a major part. The growth of the *idea* of the holy is not adequately seen with the widening use of the *word* holy. Indeed, the word 'holy' does not widen very much. It is within the word 'righteousness' that the growth is seen. 'Holiness' remains largely a word of the *cultus* but it makes a marriage with 'righteousness' (which has a noble ethical development in the Old Testament) and it is a marriage made in heaven. Jeremiah sees the consummation. He can look on to the time when Zion shall be both 'a habitation of justice' and 'a mountain of holiness'.[28]

There is no reason to doubt that there were those in Israel from its earliest beginnings to whom ethical values were dear. Even if we allow for the tendency of uncritical historians to idealize the early records of their people, we know enough of the genius of the Hebrews to find anticipation of their greatest prophets centuries before the prophets appeared. It is impossible to believe that the prophets stepped out of nothing. Most students of the history of religion would deny that they could have appeared among any other people at that time. The fine prophetic flowering, say, of the eighth century B.C., had its roots in previous ages and the soil of the ethical was the soil of their religious faith.

Both Jeremiah and Isaiah look back to the years in the desert as though the people had a purity then that they lost when they settled in Canaan and felt the pressure of the 'lesser breeds without the law'.[29] We need not dismiss all this as just another illustration of the human tendency to idealize the past. The transition from the nomadic to the settled life brings religious as well as economic problems,[30] and the cult of the baalim must have been very seductive to the newly settled Israelites, incapable, at first, of getting from the soil what the Canaanites, more skilled in husbandry, could secure. How could the Israelites help wondering if they were worshipping the wrong God? Was Yahweh but a God of war? If He was kept in the chief place, should not some place be found also for these lesser

[28] Jer 31₂₃. [29] Is 63₁₇f. Jer 2₂f.
[30] Ryder Smith, *Bible Doctrine of Society*, pp. 17ff.

C

gods of fertility? After all, civility in these circumstances costs very little. So the appeal of the baalim grew.

Little wonder that the prophets, looking back to the days when a nomadic people had none of these problems to face and when the deliverance of the Red Sea was still fresh in their mind, should regard the years in the desert as years of spiritual health and moral purity.

But what surprises an intelligent reader of the Old Testament, unacquainted with the relation of the religious and the ethical in the thought of primitive people, is the way that ritual and moral injunction jostle one another in the early law-code as though both were equally important. The laws of Israel provide numerous examples. The clearest, noblest ethical demand sits beside a trifling ceremonial requirement sharing the same divine sanction and plainly without higher warrant in the minds of those who set them down. Efforts have been made to prove that these injunctions of ceremonial purity often had some basis in plain hygiene, even though that basis has become obscured with the years. We need not contest the truth of that—in some instances and to some extent.

But the problem is not removed that way. This is the effort of a later rationalizing age. The essentially ritual and ceremonial character of these laws are what matter to us in this study. They witness in their own way to the unity in the idea of the holy which we have had in view from the beginning. In the mind of those who set them down these laws belonged together; at least, they belonged to the same 'complex' in the human mind, as they belonged with equal authority to the will of the deity who imposed them both. The rational and the non-rational in the idea of the holy appears again at this later level of development. Utterly abased mortals approaching God must learn how to come—and survive. Communion with the 'Great Other' is so truly awe-ful that the laws which regulate it can hardly be regarded as less important than the laws which regulate one's dealings with one's fellow mortals. So both appear in the codes together and only the ethical preoccupations of a modern age regard the combination as odd and call the union 'anachronistic'.

The first part of Leviticus 19 is a good instance. It begins with the solemn injunction, 'Ye shall be holy: for I the Lord your God am holy', and goes on to include ethical teaching unsurpassed and, perhaps, unparalleled in the codes of early peoples. The corners of the field are to be left unreaped at harvest time for the poor. For the sake of the poor also the vineyards must not be gleaned. Yet not for the poor only. The *stranger* is to share in that bounty too: that is, the resident foreigner, the man outside the covenant and utterly without 'rights'. The mercy of God is over *him*. Stealing, lying, and crafty trade are condemned. A man hired for a day must be paid the same evening. The deaf and the blind are to receive tender treatment, and justice is lifted above all favouritism of persons. Libel and vengefulness are condemned—even to the nursing of hate *in the heart.*

Yet, interspersed with and following these ethical regulations are rules for offering a sacrifice which is to be eaten on the day it is offered and, if any survives to the third day and is eaten then, the man who eats it has profaned 'the holy thing of the Lord' and his 'soul shall be cut off from his people'. Laws are given also on the kind of hair-cut a man must have and how his beard should be trimmed! Elsewhere, and in great detail, precise rules are laid down of the beasts which must be offered in sacrifice and how prepared and how disposed of.[31]

Within the idea of the holy in the Old Testament, a war was waged between the ritual and the ethical. It was not war to the death. Ezekiel, the third great prophet of holiness, is a great defender and expositor of ritual, though it is an exalted ritual; a ritual expressing and conserving the ethical holiness for which he stood.

Some who are passionate for the ethical values of religion, and for religion itself, have no place for ritual. They would regard all regulations concerning the cultus in early law codes as nothing but a survival of the primitive. They sometimes quote Isaiah, and his hot denunciation of ceremonies, as proof that in his concern for holiness all interest in ritual had disappeared. Did he not say:

'To what purpose is the multitude of your sacrifices unto me? saith the Lord: I am full of the burnt offerings of rams, and the fat of fed beasts; and I delight not in the blood of bullocks, or of lambs, or of he-goats. . . . Bring no more vain oblations; incense is an abomination unto me; new moon and sabbath, the calling of assemblies . . . your appointed feasts my soul hateth: they are a trouble unto me: I am weary to bear them.'[32]

But it is not certain, even in the face of this and similar denunciations, that Isaiah had no place for ritual at all. It was in the *Temple*

[31] Lev 22₁₇f.   [32] Is 1₁₁₋₁₇.

that his great vision came. Surely, it was a concern for the shrine which explains his spirited scorn of Sennacherib.[33] It was a debased, a hollow, an unspiritual cultus he denounced. He was facing the problem which the militantly devout have had to face in all ages. Symbols which express nothing. Forms from which the soul has dropped clean out. Holydays which have deteriorated into holidays. Ceremonies which express nothing but the people's eagerness for dropping their work and indulging their lower appetites.

The problem is with us still. Sir Frederick Treves, describing a Christmas Day when he was house surgeon in the London Hospital, said of the people of east London: 'Men and women were celebrating the birth of Christ by eating too much, by getting drunk and by street rioting . . .'[34]

Yet the debasing of holy days and ceremonies and symbols does not deny their fitting place and proper use. If they had no higher sanction than a craving in the mind of man, it could not be denied that something in the soul calls out for symbols and meaningful ceremony. If anyone doubts it, let him attend the funeral of a militant atheist and see a few men put a box in a hole of the earth and walk away. That is how they disposed of the remains of Charles Bradlaugh. Arthur Porritt, who was present, said:

'No prayer was said at the grave. Indeed, not a single word was uttered. The remains, placed in a light coffin, were lowered into the earth in a quite unceremonious fashion as if carrion were being hustled out of sight. . . . I came away heart-frozen. It only then dawned on me that loss of faith in the continuity of human personality after death gives death an appalling victory'.[35]

There are moments in life which demand some mannered handling. If a prayer were impossible on this occasion, having regard to Bradlaugh's conviction and wishes, the dumb awareness of many who were present that something was missing provides its own evidence that man is not wholly of the earth, earthy. Death speaks the eternities and never so much as when one seeks to silence it. Then, with awful solemnity, its silence speaks.

Nor is it only in moments as solemn as these that the human heart demands ceremony and symbols. He who would abolish symbols altogether must never again shake hands with a friend, or

[33] 2 K 19$_{20-34}$.   [34] *The Elephant Man*, p. 206.
[35] *The Best I Remember*, pp. 165 f.